BEETHOVEN'S DREAM

Also by Eric Selland:

POETRY

The Condition of Music (Sink Press, 2000)
Inventions (Mindmade Books, 2007)
Still Lifes (Hank's Original Loose Gravel Press, 2012)
Arc Tangent (Isobar Press, 2014)

TRANSLATIONS

Yoshioka Minoru, *Kusudama* (Leech Books,1991)
Takagai Hiroya, *Rush Mats* (Duration Press, 1999)
Takashi Hiraide, *The Guest Cat* (New Directions, 2014)

BEETHOVEN'S DREAM

Eric Selland

ISOBAR
PRESS

First published in 2015 by

Isobar Press
Sakura 2-21-23-202
Setagaya-ku
Tokyo 156-0053
Japan

http://isobarpress.com

ISBN 978-4-907359-10-2

COVER IMAGE:
Sketch of the Piano Sonata in A major, Op. 101,
Allegro, by Ludwig van Beethoven (detail), reproduced
from the collections of the Library of Congress.

CONTENTS

Sketches

I was thinking about how words appear as if a kind of background, strung through the landscape like pieces of shiny organic matter. The intimation of geese and other wild animals, as in water, the lagoon's green against the sky. And the shiny buildings. I did not want to talk about it. I did not want to be here. And to this comes another sense of the unavoidable. The words and their silences. Holding something, like an artisan's tools. The word 'duration' appears like a phantom across the hotel façade and then, just as suddenly, disappears.

Other requirements
Of which there are many
The blurred heights
Inform and instruct
It is almost the exact center

Where the order of exposure is disturbed

A record of locations through which the object has passed

In those days many of the old family farms remained. The house occupied the center, set among rows of fruit trees – apricot, fig, peach. The house itself was protected by a stand of shade trees meant to keep out the intense heat of the semi-desert sun. These were fast-growing trees that would grow tall and resist the ravages of summer – mainly eucalyptus and sometimes poplar, palm or cotton-wood. When the farms disappeared, only the circle of trees remained.

Let us begin with the concept of space
The first moment, where one has not yet found terms

There are a few other wrinkles
Light from the edge
Glass donut

The cries of the cedar waxwings formed
A blanket around the core of silence –
We find that we are lost.

In the distance I can see my parents' house. Higher than the high black fences surrounding it are the trees. In the cold dusk of autumn I can hear the lonely click and caw of the red-winged blackbirds. I smell the rotten odor of the carob blossoms and think about the slow turning of the seasons.

Now to return to the river
That which cannot be articulated
Something hidden or misplaced

I was walking
Listening to them speak with each other

There's something called a 'happy stop'
We can move on

Removed from the framework

One senses the gathering of time into this moment
Growth and decay

I welcome the return of the organic

To carry the question
To hold the question within oneself

The way that each of these moments depends on the other

The landscape exceeds itself

That it would be
An indication
A measure of what is

Outside history
What would it mean
To remember?

The cold sun hanging in the sky descends behind the glass buildings. The hills are near, green-gold as the day approaches solitude. An ending, free of worry. The essential clutter of existence. It is a certain burden – this Americanness. To raise the question more intently, more intimately. To process the image, which is inaccurate. One shape suggested a screaming mouth. He described it as a door, a way to leave. Exile and longing. Writing himself into the text of the times.

The return to the figure: always the same image – a woman moving in and out of focus. The body was more than its form. It's really about the pause, the small stop before breathing, where the intention flies off 'like a dove' and leaves the core. This is where work is, and where life is lived. No trace left.

I wanted to write about the tools and the wood. We establish the horizons of expectation. Finding oneself again in movement. The condition of possibility. How then will it be possible to speak? Within the sphere I perceive bodies, yet appearing in person. My father appeared to me in a dream, angrily insisting that it was he who held the cure to memory loss. On the way to the bus small pieces of paper tumble, mix together and are lost, unrecognizable. Small feet ascend the stairs. What is the function of writing. What is direction, interiority. The heart of language. At the heart of the writing is a dream. The father speaks. That I am exposed.

A field in which the orders of light turn on specific points, only to be redirected, so that we no longer see, nor understand, but are left instead with only the vague sense of an occurrence. The familiar becomes unfamiliar. Three-dimensional objects applied to canvas, each motionless vessel fixed in place. The solitary figure.

The rings of the sculpture
Open
This simultaneity of absence
And presence
The disappearing subject

I found that I had left him behind. That they belong together. Within the space of representation, the most comfortable distance between an absolute distance and an intolerable closeness is the median point. Removed from their original context. Removed from concept. Disquietude. The state of perplexity. It is also just as obvious that this falling out has happened to us. The bounded figure. The field is thus constituted inside itself as a figure of its own absence. The play of surfaces. The key is by definition missing. The way in which the indifferently many items are together without being concerned with one another.

A history of places through which one has passed. The Greeks understood tragedy as the most apt expression of the human condition. The underlying configuration. The complexities of the horizon line. The absurdities of relation.

As resolution improves, depth of focus deteriorates
Critical dimension

The boundary
Which remains unthought

I am trying to be born, but cannot find the exit. I am in a small, cramped space, a kind of netting; an underground tunnel beyond which I can see the outside world. The feet of passersby move past the range of sight. It is difficult to breathe. I squirm in an attempt to get out, but I am caught in the netting.

Properties of light
Map of the surface
That all left the source with no obstruction
A wavefront emanating from a light source will
                                    be spherical
Ripples on the surface
The closer the elements, the more repulsion
Different patterns send light through different parts
                                    of the lens
How does my image change now that the aberrations
                                    are changing

The story goes on in starts and stops, scattered episodes moving forward toward an unknowable future. Fragmented dreams. The disappearance of genre. I've written whole novels in my head and forgotten them. A dim light. It embraces necessity. It rectifies to adjust. I too was dreaming. Alternate beginnings. Alternate lives.

I am a concert pianist. The hall is filled with members of the city's elite, eagerly awaiting my performance. I see by the sheet music placed on the piano that I am to play a piece by Mendelssohn. Suddenly I realize that I don't play the piano – it's been years since I took any lessons, and not only that, I don't even like Mendelssohn. Quickly I concoct an experimental performance work using appropriated language supplied by the audience. I am saved. Later I begin unloading the baggage of the wealthy down the stairs backstage.

That there are things, at least in the time and place of this story, that remain unspoken. I am looking for an image, for a word. I am looking for historical facts. That which is profoundly hidden. Only I can understand my own condition. He speaks to us in a language we no longer understand.

They found a little man in the root of a tree
His mouth open as if about to speak

The shape of the mouth
The human form

He was asleep or he was dead
Like a dried root

This is man
Drawn out across the top

Along the length of the wafer stage
The robot arms are nearly falling off

To put the table at the center

Something wrong with my voice
Something caught in my voice

Some interesting effects
Can be obtained
Light pictures on the wall

Holding in the object
Against the gaze
The world presses in on them

Maps are dramatically different
It's a work in progress
Of practical residence

We receive a package of exotic gifts from China, one of these being a large horned lizard that will attack upon being approached. Before awakening I see the animal, strangely human-like, boxing. Weaving in and out, arms outstretched, it stands and bares its teeth.

On a human scale
Hitting one point on the mirror
The dream merely ends

So it was a painting about light
All light and reflection

The linear
The boundary of its truth

A collage of the real
The material of the world

The glass slips over the edge of the field
The bottle casts a shadow
Continuing into the present century
There are multiple fields
The world of things
Outside the painting

I feel differently at different times
And then I am another person
The question leaves a trace in the mind

One could describe the house as a refuge
The arc of the possible

Mostly old things
You thought you'd left behind

The translational axis
Exile of the egg
The moving axis of rotation always has the same
                                        direction in space
Defined as displacement

Truth will be available only as experience, as process
The confusion between item and category

Define authenticity
Using the methodology until it reaches its logical
                                        end-point

The failure of the work
The signs indicating its former habitation

One discovers the light on every plane

The apartment consisted of two small rooms, the light breaking through the clouds. Three persimmons and a Japanese pumpkin on the cutting board, cherry or maple I think. But the art of correspondence is lost. Each was irreducibly personal – connected the town in a vast underground web. He was forever in doubt, the hand twisted back upon itself. He could not easily forget the past, the human scale. This was his ambivalent nature. It reflects while you are reflecting.

He began struggling to piece together the fragments of a man. The lines themselves were a kind of becoming. Something struggling to be born. As in the Kantian idea, the infinite overflowing of horizons. I have regard for the face itself even in speaking of it. The task is not without difficulty. The texture of everyday life.

The death of place
And the emergence of the new
The mutability of categories
The text's refusal

Impromptu
Exposition / Fantasia / Coda

One creates the first
Of a certain size
Then it spreads out
Not what I pictured
We have been struggling
Not circles
But more like tears

From the direction of the capital
A red glow lit up the sky

Gathering momentum
The train comes through

Hidden in the dim light
The face moves forward
Then turns toward the exit

This is how it falls apart
In the tunnel
With the blackened hand

Technologies of the self
It remains in the system
Separated from his own moment

A more complex mechanism was identified
It's like a beautiful prison
Autobiography

Falling back within oneself
There is no place
What were the conditions

In the dialogue, the philosopher implies a dead end
The quest for experience
The crisis of agency
The fallen world of objects

It is a room we close off, and nobody can see it. The sickness returns, mathematically speaking, spreads, envelops. A pain still reverberates in the mind. Suddenly the paintings were brighter, moving out into broad vistas and continuing in that vein until his eventual suicide. Thus, the change which is in understanding arrives at its own matter, at the interior. Not in the interior of the object of understanding. It is in itself the opposite; the brief mention of a movement. Flatness may now monopolize everything, providing a transverse region of significantly increased flexibility. So color was after all a sort of clarity. How to make color speak. Lost in the image pattern. Is there a problem with theatricality? The physics of perception, unlived, limned.

In his manner of dress, for instance, he shows a perfunctory approach to the age. He enters the black sedan. What is this nature? There is a strange beauty in the fact of the accumulation itself. Remembering and forgetting. He turns in the dream to find C turning towards him, her face a conjunction of brevities, eyes suggesting a meaning. There is a much more broad-ranging mechanism at work. Once he introduced the parallel he withdrew. There were several attempts at simplification. We had been speaking amongst ourselves about electricity, animal magnetism. Transference, therefore, is quite appropriate. Now comes the most interesting stage of the process of cognition. Understood primarily in spatial terms – the scheme of departing and returning; being itself, who speaks and can be spoken of.

The way intervening space forms an energy of its own between two bodies. The secret of the dance. He lived in an imperfect world of fragments. A room within a room. It's as if you could walk way inside the painting. What does one do? Shapes bearing a distant resemblance. The shattered form. A window. So you could map this like points on a scale. I am in the picture. Shapes abruptly shift in velocity and depth. Images lose themselves in other images.

The force of the sacrifice lies in the entanglement
He began to empty out the landscapes of the last few years

The blades press against each other with great force
An excess which cannot be grasped

He encountered great lights on movable platforms. He devised a thin metal arm that could attach itself to the arc of night. He attempted to regulate the reflection of light. Even sleep remained open – transparently so. In it he saw a ship coming to rest within a great space amongst the trees. The occasion. It is a question of modality.

Here we are confronted with a restaging: after passing through the center of himself, the walls, multicolored, breathe in and out, undulate to an unknown brightness. Thus words function properly. I can't help but feel sick. The icon also is incomplete. Word and thing, orphans, the other – for an instant it is all on the table. And the wood, too, is present. Where does the opening of the body lead?

All I have done is to wish to say something

The child is there
Or not there
The closed chamber
The trace

Beethoven's Dream

Last night I dreamed. Although no music was performed, yet it was a musical dream.

Ludwig van Beethoven, *Letters*

In the myth of the self there is a curious plotline, runs from the miniscule to the grandiose. There are the things of life that are real. The action in a sonata arising from the material. Changes that are still more profound. The opening of every beat.

Where do I start?
Perhaps with narrow escapes
A question in the mind

Much is required
The path of light passes through the center
One knows only hunger for certain

Our procedure has, in a sense, been circular. It is this future word. Impersonal, yet occurring just where we hear it, and where there is music. A little path that goes off into the woods, like an illustration in a children's book. It is most near to us. How the objects form a set of overly heavy, discolored ensembles. They are set out in the room as if on a great plain in the desert of another country. They are broken or perhaps a bit offset. There is no straight line. I draw a path through the woods along the crest of a hill. I add some color, but abruptly stop. The sounds migrating toward the mouth like sediments. To recompose the image. The imagined self.

Later he will go out again, but he will be changed. We must give up everything. The moment of release. The ascent. The sense of dislocation. There are all these different forces at work. Using the point where light returns from beyond the region where it is blocked. A power comes to reside in an object. Identity emerged as a cluster of unstable boundaries. That which is beyond description.

The visitor, neither expected nor invited.

He proposed yet a third kind of separation. It's all absorbed into the background. A kind of confluence of wavefronts that when detected forms a circle. It would have to have an individual language. The meaning of a word can be troublesome. The universal and the particular. They meet at the vanishing point. Each is alone in the empty street. Light pierces the shadows of the buildings. One turns away. I cannot turn away. The notions of excess and supplement. The reality is too large for us to take in.

The cup contains a liquid
The substance of the return

We are now conducting experiments in which the prism will break; in which we see multiplicities of broken history. A force occurs or is applied. The head implodes or is merely dulled, like the drone of afternoon television. In either case we see or do not see, and after a while it's all over. The function of a room. A further distance. A second level of alienation.

I am trying to come to a point. To maintain a single form. The tragic collision. To the extent that it becomes appearance. The real gift is time. Where we are again confronted with great complexity. The machinery begins, and the night begins, restless, interweaving. Thus the path followed by the electron turns out to be a parabola. The deflection of the electron from its initial path. He required the closeness of memory. An object moves from a point in space. Thus potential. Action or loss. Short, fragmented sounds are complete in themselves. To the degree of which the possible is approached. It's a matter of the choices made.

To strip down the thing so as to retain only its naked reality.

The thought of a gravitational field. The source that triggers the signal. I hear a door opening in the darkness. I hear the machines turning, humming in the hollow distance. I follow the music, rising now to an absurd rhythm. The instruments spring open and collapse, like the voice with its resemblances. The top of the waveform extends beyond the boundaries of the window. It is difficult to be entirely consistent. As soon as one thinks one has arrived at a simple rule, exceptions begin to appear. I have listened to him for a long time. A line drawn to the infinite future and the infinite past. This should be governed by certain underlying principles – yet just what are these principles?

To overcome the text
The image like a signature

In outward appearance alone the board moves
Only settings differ
Shadow setting
We must disentangle the various embedded structures
His only known escape from the tyranny of the tiny figure
The gaze of the spectator

The tyranny of the perfect sentence
Shadow image, dark field
I have a face in mind
But I'm not sure it's the right one
The stillness of being
Escape from perfection

Uncertainty
Bears the burden of meaning
Another layer of identity
All the faces I put on and take off
What is a transcendental field?
It doesn't refer to an object or belong to a subject

Whoever wants to be first must be last of all
As increase or decrease
It is a life, and nothing else
Passage to other, to becoming
Or an object falling outside the plane
A single voice

See, I have inscribed you on the palms of my hands
The pattern of energy striking the surface
The error of incidence
The image travels through infinite energy to a small space
Where the isolated line peaks
The higher orders of light

The wound is a higher actuality
The object model
Spatial coordinates
A plane or a field
Possible form
I am looking for a word

The device is disassembled and placed below the stage
The mirror drops onto the plane
In order to enter the text of his life
A question of the particular
A scene of expansion or condensation
Coming into contact with an object

Where person becomes landscape
Definition of a door
That which remains attached
It is dark inside and difficult to move
Pull out the front rack and fold back the handles
History was always a work in progress

In general I am satisfied with the symphony
A symphony like any other
Things around which the attention gathers
Pieces of life, pieces of music
The grotesque in two movements
The transparent tips of the steeples

The painting must extract the figure. Visions of bodies plunging through the tunnel – blackness, a kind of color. The micro-organisms gather in the brightest place. Color; sensation. Finally the words return beyond image. Suggestion of thought. The bus crawls through the valley like a huge caterpillar. Waiting. Deprivation. The andante. Tragedy or relief, now the instance – erasure of memory.

Now figure becomes person. Particles providing the nuts and bolts. It is like the emergence of another world. The hand intervenes. Another order. But the body is not simply waiting for something. It is a trajectory. Chaos, or what is art. I have often tried to talk about painting, or about life ... the unspeakable. We dream, sometimes of history, of bits and pieces of the house as it is dismantled.

It tends to fall away. The interior forces. Vast fields of color in which the figure detaches itself, forms an armature in the infinity of a field, and in another way as passage. The figure itself is isolated. To delineate person. A circular space. A story slips into the space between two figures. Clearly the problem is more complicated than this.

A return to the elements
What is happening or is about to happen
The role of spectacle

Shadows separate to reveal shadow on shadow. Sound of
footsteps through the empty street. The city is deserted.
Why April suddenly? A lingering cold oozes up out of
the low-lying areas. Deformities such as warping are not
uncommon. Imperfections of the wafer surface occur due
to temperature, thus contributing to lower yield. The
material of the figure.

To dismantle the face
This is the reality of becoming

Speech, dialogue, and conversation. Everything is becoming a part, sucked into the larger machinery, unstopping. One can feel lost or left behind, but it all goes on anyway. Now to the illustrations. The text, the solution to the puzzle. Let us present a series of examples: the nose disappearing from the face leaving a gap, a question open in the absent expression. There are no faces, only signs. I would like to say I am lost, but I am here, exactly here. When light is liberated and becomes independent of forms. As if the picture had its own life. We seem to glimpse at that precise moment outside time the external world, its varied motifs, and yet we do not understand.

The landscape flows outside the limits of representation
The eye and the hand
The larger theme

The end of all things seemed to lead to just such a point. Musical examples, like tables, carry something already at work. World as artifact. Parts of the city are sealed off. Dissipation reaches an extreme point. The characters appearing in the window. He gets up and walks away. The membrane covering the field like a vacant breath.

Behind the glass is an unevenness
The face of a man
Without illusions
He has come to see
How ridiculous time is
The things that are actually there
And how they disperse
Or gradually decay
The reverse of their bright surfaces

There was no particular plan
The almost imperceptible shift from movement to rest

The egg reveals
Just this state
Rhythmic unity
The ground upon which
One stands, dazed, somewhat bemused
A great mouth opens up
Collapse into abbreviated form
Invasion, succession, filtering, and tipping
Translation and migration

Now we are grasping repeatedly the sentence and its meaning, always open to interpretation, the handles located on the side doors, groping in the dark. In the darkened room deformation is obtained in the form at rest. We must consider the special case. Music, for its part, is faced with the same task. Objects whose action decomposes, always as victims of invisible forces. The screams behind the curtain.

The first invisible forces are those of isolation. There is the force of changing time. The existence of a substance. The intersection of two black sides of a square. Most profoundly they have influenced me in ways that have never met with the page. It is characteristic to pass through different levels. Like a series of awakenings. Grasping, taking hold. The text itself betrays the rhythm of the relation. Reveals a surface where the deeper wounds gradually emerge and become visible in the unpacked boxes, the old furniture and oriental curios. A sense of place. But would I have the courage to speak? In that context, they are all present. What we have to define.

I think that this thing was an absolute thing, a large part of man in that it was lost. The painting was never complete. I am searching for a real apple. The only true thing. He divides the domain into two parts. Equal and unequal probabilities. So the act of painting is always shifting. Separation. The limit. The effects of time from loading to exposure. It is easy to see in that way. Joyous time of decomposition. What does the act consist of?

Plato's cave, the shadows projected against the wall. The eye collapses into incandescence – into trough. Bend or fill. Runs the finger along the spine, extending on either side. It is like the emergence of another world. I am no closer to understanding than before. A tempered use of the diagram. Using the pedal to modify the pitches. Tonality happens. A tree stands in continual reproach to human culture. Imagining other selves.

Yesterday, everything was done in a consecutive way, so it was my 'exclusive province'. In other words, I was very comfortable. The whole idea, really, is to return to that place. Synthesis is thus an analytic of elements. One can also make a combination that will yield a message. Thus we cannot be content. I think we're ripe for an image. The wire supports holding the aperture are designed to prevent refraction. The photograph can rarely escape this limit. The primary function of the filter. What separates and unites.

I am interested in a lot of things: how birds sing in the magnetic field, the waking dream, what is occurring in the eyes and the nature of light. That's crucial. To show this as surface. It seems as though speed is essential to thought before it catches up with itself. We don't really have the language to talk about these things. Finally the outer limits are revealed. The buried city. It seemed there were hesitant passages. The background remained unresolved. Sometimes the subject is isolated in space, like a cowboy. The deformed body escapes from itself.

He added a tiny boat on the horizon. 'There is no boat in the painting', she said. Each had a distinctive character. During the harvest, old shoes are worn down, motifs are repeated. I never moved it from the block. Leaving the factory late one night, I step out into the dark cool to see an old man all alone in the empty lot pulling a set of bagpipes out of the trunk of his car. The sound of the pipes warming up, whining like a dying animal, echoes in the industrial sleep. The basic elements: an enclosed space and hesitant speech, in which the participants never fail to misunderstand one another. The state of perplexity.

We have established a level of uncertainty
Echoes like envelopes
The dead arrive slowly
They are held up in traffic
On their way over the bridge

That the allegretto had been conceived years earlier
Creation, fracture and assembly
With all the voices in my head
A face emerges
The dactylic sighing figure

I looked out of the window. In it there is already perfection. For a moment I am awake. Elsewhere things happen. Uniformity, history. But which of course begs the question. The signature contained clear signs of disruption. One hears the adagio constantly. I am not certain of the meaning. Recovering from an undefined position. That it can escape, even if there is interference.

A Note on Sources

Major sources: *Beethoven's Letters* (Dover Books); Walter Benjamin, *The Task of the Translator;* Thomas P. Brockelman, *The Frame and the Mirror: On Collage and the Postmodern;* Gilles Deleuze, *Francis Bacon: The Logic of the Figure;* Clement Greenberg, various articles and essays; Rosalind Krauss, *The Originality of the Avant-Garde and Other Myths;* Maynard Solomon, *Beethoven, Beethoven Essays* and *Late Beethoven: Music, Thought, Imagination;* Mark Stevens and Annalyn Swan, *de Kooning: An American Master;* Virginia Woolf, *The Hours;* plus samples of technical documentation on optics and semiconductor manufacturing equipment.

www.ingramcontent.com/pod-product-compliance
Lightning Source LLC
Chambersburg PA
CBHW031213090426
42736CB00009B/897